CASTOR AND POLLUX

Borgo Press Books by FRANK J. MORLOCK

Castor and Pollux and Other Opera Libretti (Editor)
The Chevalier d'Éon and Other Short Farces (Editor)
Chuzzlewit
Congreve's Comedy of Manners
Crime and Punishment
Cyrano and Molière: Five Plays by or About Molière (Editor)
Falstaff (with William Shakespeare, John Dennis, and William Kendrick)
Fathers and Sons
The Idiot
Isle of Slaves and Other Plays (Editor)
Jurgen
Justine
The Londoners & The Green Carnation: Two Plays
Lord Jim
The Madwoman of Beresina and Other Napoleonic Plays (Editor)
Notes from the Underground
Oblomov
Old Creole Days
Outrageous Women: Lady Macbeth and Other French Plays (Editor)
Peter and Alexis
The Princess Casamassima
A Raw Youth
The Stendhal Hamlet Scenarios and Other Shakespearean Shorts from the French (Editor)
Two Voltairean Plays: The Triumvirate; and, Comedy at Ferney (editor)
The Widow's Husband; and, Porthos in Search of an Outfit: Two Dumasian Comedies (Editor)
Zeneida & The Follies of Love & The Cat Who Changed into a Woman: Two Plays (Editor)

CASTOR AND POLLUX

AND OTHER OPERA LIBRETTI

FRANK J. MORLOCK,

EDITOR

THE BORGO PRESS
MMXIII

CASTOR AND POLLUX

Copyright © 2003, 2013 by Frank J. Morlock

FIRST EDITION

Published by Wildside Press LLC

www.wildsidebooks.com

DEDICATION

For My Grandsons,
Miles, Nicholas, and Sebastian,
with Love from Grandpa

CONTENTS

CASTOR AND POLLUX, by Pierre Bernard 9
CAST OF CHARACTERS. 10
ACT I, Scene 1 12
ACT II, Scene 2. 22
ACT III, Scene 3 29
ACT III, Scene 4 32
ACT IV, Scene 5 39
ACT IV, Scene 6 44
ACT V, Scene 7. 52
ACT V, Scene 8. 60
PENELOPE, by Jean-François Martonel. 63
CAST OF CHARACTERS. 64
ACT I, Scene 1 65
ACT II, Scene 2. 83
ACT II, Scene 3. 89
ACT III, Scene 4 103
ACT III, Scene 5 120

SAPPHO, by Émile Augier 127
CAST OF CHARACTERS: 128
ACT I, Scene 1 129
ACT II, Scene 2. 147
ACT II, Scene 3. 168
ACT III, Scene 4 170
ACT IV, Scene 5 191
ABOUT THE EDITOR 201

CASTOR AND POLLUX
BY PIERRE BERNARD,
Music by Jean-Philippe Rameau

CAST OF CHARACTERS

POLLUX, son of Jupiter and Leda, King of Sparta

CASTOR, son of Tyndareus and Leda

TELAIRE, daughter of the Sun, sister of Phoebe

PHOEBE, daughter of the Sun, sister of Telaire

JUPITER

MERCURY

CLEONA, Phoebe's confidant

HIGH PRIEST OF JUPITER

TROUPE OF PRIESTS

TWO SPARTANS

HEBE, dancing character

CELESTIAL PLEASURES and FOLLOWERS of Phoebe

A FEMALE FOLLOWER of Phoebe

A TROUPE OF MAGICIANS

A TROUPE OF DEMONS AND MONSTERS

THE FURIES

THE HAPPY SHADES

A HAPPY FEMALE SHADE

THE PEOPLE OF SPARTA

THE GENIES who preside over the Planets and Constellations

ACT I
SCENE 1

The stage represents the Palace of the King of Sparta, prepared to celebrate a marriage.

CLEONA:

Marriage crowns your sister, Pollux is marrying Telaire.

This pompous preparation announces his happiness,

But I hear Phoebe, who's sighing.

PHOEBE:

My heart isn't envious of such a glorious fate.

Another voice is making itself heard within it.

Ah, how unambitious it is!

Perhaps it would be less tender.

Daughters of the God of Day, with what diverse presents

Heaven marked our share!

I received the ability to evoke Hell,

How much nicer what Telaire received!

She commands hearts where my art can do nothing;

A glance from her makes everything possible.

I can only shock what she makes sensitive.

How much her power exceeds mine!

How the Universe finds her beautiful.

I pardon that to her attractions.

But that the ingrate Castor abandoned me for her,

Now that's what my heart will never forgive him for.

CLEONA:

Marriage with the King, which is going to break their chain,

Must restore hope to you of securing your lover.

PHOEBE:

She will have his regrets, I will have only the pain

Of still vainly hoping.

And if the King gives into the tears of his brother,

The object which causes his torment?

You see what I fear; here's what I hope.

Cleona, at this fatal moment,

To avenge my offended passion,

I am keeping a rival for them

And I can dispose of the furors of Lincaeus.

His love which they are outraging is quite ready to burst out.

He wants to carry Telaire away from this palace.

I see her. Her triumph increases my martyrdom.

Let's think of avoiding her.

(Phoebe leaves with Cleona.)

TELAIRE:

(entering) Burst out, my just regrets,

In a moment, alas! I'll have to control them.

Henceforth Heaven will part me

From the sweetness that pleases me.

In vain, Glory unites all the attractions it has

For a god who adores me, and forces me to fear him.

Love hurled other features;

These honors that I flee see only the excess

Of a passion I cannot extinguish.

Burst out, my just regrets, etc.

(Enter Castor.)

CASTOR:

Ah! I shall die satisfied, I am seeing your allures again.

TELAIRE:

Prince, do you still dare to speak to me of tenderness?

CASTOR:

Our farewells are permitted.

TELAIRE:

Oughtn't you

To spare them my weakness?

CASTOR:

When I had for this farewell the admission of your spouse,

When you are going to be ravished from me;

Cruel one, do you reproach me

For the last pleasure of my life?

My brother's seen my tears and, far from hiding them,

I let him see all my passion.

Pity spoke to him, and seemed to touch him,

But love more powerful distracted his soul.

Fulfill his happiness, I will leave these parts

Without complaining of you, without accusing my brother.

Have I complained except to the gods?

TELAIRE:

You're leaving?

CASTOR:

I am imposing a necessary exile on myself.

In these eyes, masters of my fate,

I've found life a hundred times.

When hope is ravished from me

I will find death there a hundred times.

TELAIRE:

And the King will permit this inhuman flight?

No, his heart is too generous.

CASTOR:

Making his happiness softens my pain.

You pity me, he loves me, and I am leaving very happy.

(Pollux, who's been observing them, appears at this moment.)

POLLUX:

No, stay, Castor, it's I who order you to.

Love and friendship impose the law on you.

Calm the unease into which your soul's abandoning itself.

To keep you near me,

The hand that owes faith to me

Is the chain that I am giving you.

CASTOR:

O blessings that I adore!

TELAIRE:

O Grandeur that astonishes me!

POLLUX:

I know all that I am losing.

Castor will do justice to my love.

He can better judge the price of sacrifice

By the torments he has suffered.

(The suite of the King and the people enter.)

POLLUX:

(to the people) These preparations were destined for me.

I was making them my supreme happiness.

Let their faces be crowned

With these flowers that were to decorate my diadem.

Of two objects that I love

I am making two happy lovers.

CHORUS OF SPARTANS:

Let's sing of the burgeoning victory

Of a hero who is subduing Love.

If virtue is triumphing on this fine day,

Love will lose nothing of his glory.

(They dance.)

CASTOR:

What happiness reigns in my soul!

Love, have you ever

Hurled such beautiful darts?

With the hands of friendship you are crowning my passion!

Love, have you ever

Hurled such beautiful darts?

(They dance.)

A SPARTAN:

(entering) Leave these sports, run to arms!

Lincaeus is attacking this palace.

Jealous Phoebe is guiding his darts.

CHORUS:

Let's run to arms.

(As they separate to fight at the two sides of the stage, the noise of the attackers can be heard.)

CHORUS:

Let's go to dissipate these alarms.

To arms.

TELAIRE:

(to Castor) You are leaving me!

Stop, Castor, stop!

THE DIFFERENT CHORUSES:

Let's fight, let's attack, attack, fight!

A LONE VOICE:

Let's kidnap Telaire.

TELAIRE:

Ah! What furor inspires them!

(After a great uproar of battle, Lincaeus forces down the gates of the palace and appears at the head of his followers. Castor, who has left the stage, returns to fight him; he is rebuffed and falls in the wings under the blows of Lincaeus; during the battle, Telaire, who wants to hurl herself into the melee, is restrained by her women. Suddenly a profound silence.)

A VOICE:

Castor, alas! Castor has fallen under his blows!

CHORUS OF SPARTANS:

O irreparable loss!

O terrifying misfortune.

TELAIRE:

(as she falls into the arms of her servants) I am dying.

CHORUS:

Pollux, avenge us!

(The noise of battle recommences; Lincaeus reappears and crosses the stage, attacked by Pollux, who fights him, chases him, and pursues him.)

CURTAIN

ACT II
SCENE 2

The stage represents the sepulchers of the kings of Sparta; it's a somber forest, where several monuments lit by sepulchral lamps are revealed. In the principal place is a great Mausoleum raised for the funeral of Castor and surrounded by wailing people.

CHORUS OF SPARTANS:

Let all wail,

Let all join,

Let's prepare, let's raise eternal monuments

To the most unlucky of lovers:

Let neither our love nor his name ever perish;

Let all wail.

TELAIRE:

(appearing in the greatest mourning; and going to cast herself at the foot of the mausoleum)

Sad preparations, pale torches,

Day more frightful than the night,

Lugubrious stars of tombs,

No, I shall not see anything but your funereal lights.

You who see my heart dismayed,

Father of the day, O Sun! O my Father!

I no longer wish a blessing that Castor has lost,

And I renounce your light.

Sad preparation, etc.

(Phoebe appears.)

TELAIRE:

Cruel one, in what places are you coming?

Are you daring to again insult

The Manes of a hero who perished through your blows?

PHOEBE:

Leave to the love that's devouring me

The care of punishing a crime that I abhor.

It speaks to me of it more than your wrath.

You are weeping for the most tender love

But his destiny may still depend on the two of us.

With a word you can restore him to life.

TELAIRE:

What must be done? Order.

PHOEBE:

Sacrifice your love

And my art will force Hell to return him to us.

TELAIRE:

Yes, I impose the law on myself.

Let him live, so that for him your passion can reveal itself.

PHOEBE:

You wish it.

TELAIRE:

Hasten; I am ceding to my rival

The love with which he is burning for me.

(One hears a warrior symphony and songs of victory.)

CHORUS:

(Behind the stage) Triumph, vengeance.

TELAIRE:

It's the conquering king who's advancing.

PHOEBE:

He has avenged our ill deeds, we must repair them.

(Phoebe leaves.)

(Enter Pollux, with Spartans, athletes, and combatants, bearing trophies and spoils from enemies.)

POLLUX:

(to the people) Folks, cease to sigh.

No, it's no longer tears that the Manes demand;

It's blood they are expecting.

And that fatal blood's been shed;

Lincaeus has been sacrificed.

ALL THE CHORUSES:

Let Hell applaud

New concerts.

Let a plaintive shade rejoice.

The scream of vengeance is the song of Hell.

POLLUX:

(to Telaire) Princess, such a victory

Ought to soften for you the horror of this day.

TELAIRE:

Vengeance flatters glory

But doesn't console love.

Prince, a ray of hope is presenting itself to my eyes.

The power of Phoebe can fulfill our hope

And ravish Castor from Hell.

POLLUX:

No, it's in vain that she attempts it,

And it's still up to me to reunite your fetters.

To the feet of Jupiter I will go to make myself heard.

The god who gave me life

Can return it to my brother.

To the tears of his son that he observes so tenderly,

Can he give his love?

TELAIRE:

Ah! Prince! Dare to attempt all:

Reveal to the immortals that your fates are joined.

Jupiter in the Heavens is the God of Thunder

And Pollux on earth

Will be the god of friendship.

Revive the ashes of an unfortunate brother.

Tear him from the tomb, prevent me from descending into it.

Triumph with your passion, be the support of him.

Render him alive to the one he loves.

That will reveal, even to Jupiter,

That you are worthy of him.

POLLUX:

(to the people) Resume your songs of victory.

Let my triumph embellish these parts.

Occupy Telaire and charm her beautiful eyes

With the spectacle of my glory.

(Pollux leaves. The stage lights up. the tombs are covered with trophies and spoils of enemies. March of warriors. Entry and staged fight of athletes and gladiators.)

AN ATHLETE:

Blare proud trumpets;

Make the glory of our heroes

Shine in these abodes.

With songs of victory,

Let's trouble the repose

Of echoes.

Let's sing of nothing but glory.

Blare proud trumpets;

Make the glory of our heroes

Shine in these abodes.

(Spartan women mix in the celebration of the warriors, crowning the conquerors and forming a Diversion of rejoicing to celebrate the victory of Pollux.)

CURTAIN

ACT III
SCENE 3

The stage represents the vestibule of the Temple of Jupiter where Pollux must make sacrifices.

POLLUX:

(alone) Present of gods, sweet charm of humans,

O divine friendship, come penetrate our souls;

Hearts enlightened by your flames

With pure pleasures have only serene days.

It's in your charming nets that all rejoice.

Time adds yet one more luster to your beauty.

Love bequeaths you constancy

And you would be lusty

If man had his innocence.

Present of gods, etc. (the Temple opens and the priests come out)

But the Temple has opened and the High Priest is coming forward.

(The High Priest of Jupiter enters, followed by his suite and the people.)

HIGH PRIEST:

The sovereign of gods

Is going to appear in these abodes

In all the dazzle of his power.

Tremble, respect his presence,

Flee, curious mortals.

It's only through flames and the voice of thunder

That he announces himself on earth

And the dazzle of his glorious face

Is seen only by the gods.

Let the mere name of this supreme god

Freeze all hearts with respect and terror.

Flee and tremble

Let's flee and tremble ourselves.

CHORUS OF PRIESTS:

Let's flee and tremble ourselves.

(The people and the priests leave.)

ACT III
SCENE 4

The set changes. Jupiter appears in a dazzling palace seated on a throne, surrounded by his glory.

POLLUX:

(at Jupiter's feet) My voice is raised in trembling up to you,

Powerful master of the world.

With a single glance, dissipate my terror

And calm my profound sorrow.

O my father, hear my prayers.

Henceforth the immortality which enchains me

Is for your son only a terrible torture.

Castor is no more, and my vengeance is vain

If your sovereign voice

Doesn't return him to a happier life.

O my father, hear my prayers.

JUPITER:

My son, how his return would have charms for me,

How sweet it would be for me to think of it,

But Hell has laws that I cannot force

And fate forbids me to respond to your tears.

POLLUX:

Ah! Leave me alone to pierce right up to the somberest shores.

Under my feet I will open the caverns of the earth.

I will go brave Pluto; I will go seek the dead.

To the light of your thunder

I will enchain Cerberus, and more worthy of the heavens,

I will again see Castor, and my father, and the gods.

JUPITER:

I wanted to hide from you the fate that threatens you.

You can break the fetters of an unfortunate brother

If you descend into Hell.

But it is ordered that the reward for your audacity

Is that you must take his place.

Your eternal life, your beautiful life,

Are very worthy of envy.

POLLUX:

No, I can't bear life,

If Castor doesn't share the course of it with me.

I will see my brother again; he will see Telaire!

Each instant that I am breathing here

Is a blessing that I am stealing from his amorous heart.

JUPITER:

Before giving in to the zeal which inspires you

Behold what you are losing in the heavens.

Pleasures, charms of my empire,

Pleasures, you make the gods

Triumph over a god who sighs.

(The Celestial Pleasures led by Hebe enter dancing, they surround Pollux. Jupiter withdraws. Hebe and the Celestial Pleasures hold garlands of flowers with which they want to enchain Pollux.)

CHORUS OF CELESTIAL PLEASURES:

(dancing around Pollux)

Young immortal, where are you off to?

Ah! Can you not know us?

Can a god be without us?

Can a god cease to be?

POLLUX:

All the dazzle of Olympia is revived in vain.

Heaven and supreme happiness

Are in places where one loves,

Are in places where one is loved.

SMALL CHORUS:

Let Hebe, with ever fresh flowers,

Forge your eternal chains.

(They dance.)

A SERVING GIRL OF HEBE:

Here's the pleasant

Asylum of the gods.

Experience Heaven's

Durable peace.

More pleasures

Than desires,

Chains

Without pains,

And beautiful life

Counted out forever

With our loves.

If one sighs,

It's without martyrdom.

Is one charmed?

All please alike.

They say they're in love,

They're loved in return.

SMALL CHORUS:

Let Hebe, with ever fresh flowers,

Forge your eternal chains.

POLLUX:

Ah! But for the trouble in which I see myself,

I would be faithful to you charming pleasures.

But in the excess of my mortal sorrow,

What do pleasures want from me?

(Hebe's dance.)

A SERVANT OF HEBE:

Let our sports

Fulfill your wishes.

Follow Hebe, so that your youth

Ceaselessly

Is reborn

To be forever happy.

The most brilliant grandeur

Is not the attraction that tempts us.

Come, see, experience

Celestial sensuality.

We love, even Jupiter

Is only happy when he's in love.

Love, surrender, follow

The blessings that are reserved for you.

(The dancing recommences; the Celestial Pleasures make new efforts to stop Pollux.)

POLLUX:

If I am breaking your pleasant chains,

I am sparing the gods my shame and my sighs.

I am descending into Hell to forget my pains,

And Castor, reborn, will taste your pleasures.

(Pollux breaks the garlands of flowers with which he is enchained, and steals away from the pleasures who follow him.)

CURTAIN

ACT IV
SCENE 5

The stage represents the entrance to Hell, whose passage is guarded by monsters, Specters, and Demons; it's a cavern that ceaselessly vomits flames.

PHOEBE:

(alone) Spirits, support my power.

Come, fly, fulfill my hope,

Descend to the somber shore.

It's necessary to ravish a shade.

(Spirits and Magic Powers appear at Phoebe's call; she performs enchantments.)

PHOEBE:

Assemble, second my passion,

Combat the fury of monsters from Hell.

CHORUS:

Let's combat the fury of monsters from Hell.

PHOEBE:

Increase your charms,

Penetrate this retreat

Impenetrable to light,

Increase your charms,

Borrow the features of love

To have stronger arms.

CHORUS:

Increase our charms.

PHOEBE:

But, what do I see?

(She notices Mercury descending; Pollux appears at the same time.)

MERCURY:

Phoebe, you are making vain efforts,

See the useless effect of your enchantments.

The son of Jupiter alone will have the advantage

Of penetrating somber shores.

PHOEBE:

Ah! Prince, where are you rushing to?

POLLUX:

I am flying to Victory,

Who must crown my labors.

The path to Hell, beneath the steps of a hero,

Becomes the path of glory.

PHOEBE:

Let me anticipate your steps;

Let me brave all obstacles;

The miracle of triumphing over death

Is owed to Love.

POLLUX:

Let's go, Mercury, to where you are taking me.

The passion I'm experiencing on this day

Loans more rapid wings to my friendship

Than those of love.

(Pollux intends to enter the cavern; all the monsters and demons leave Hell to defend the passage.)

MERCURY, POLLUX, AND PHOEBE:

Fall, return to slavery,

Halt, furious demons.

POLLUX:

Open to me this frightful passage.

PHOEBE AND MERCURY:

Open to him this frightful passage.

POLLUX:

And respect the son of the most powerful of gods.

PHOEBE AND MERCURY:

And respect the son of the most powerful of gods.

CHORUS OF DEMONS:

Let's leave slavery,

Let's shut this frightful passage.

(Dance of Demons trying to terrify Pollux.)

CHORUS OF DEMONS:

Let's break all our fetters,

Let's shake the earth,

Let's torch the air,

Against the fire of thunder

Let the fires of Hell

Declare war.

Let's break all our fetters.

Jupiter himself

Ought to be subdued

To the supreme power

Of united Hell.

This bold god,

Does he want his son

To dethrone his brother?

Let's break all our fetters, etc.

(The Demons continue their dance and increase their efforts to ward off Pollux. The Furies come out of Hell armed with torches and serpents. Pollux battles the Demons. Mercury strikes them with his Caduceus, and sinks with Pollux into the Cavern. Phoebe, who is unable to follow them, gives in to despair.)

ACT IV
SCENE 6

The stage represents the Elysian Fields. One sees the River Lethe which snakes through this delightful abode. Some happy shades appear to wander in the distance and come to meet Castor.

CASTOR:

Abode of eternal peace,

Won't you calm my impatient soul?

Love pursues me with its darts even in these parts.

Castor sees only his lover

And you are wasting all your attractions.

Abode, etc.

How sweet that murmur is! How fresh that shade is!

With these touching harmonies sensuality enchants me,

Everything laughs, everything foresees my desire,

And yet I still conceive hopes.

Abode, etc.

CHORUS OF HAPPY SHADES:

(enter dancing)

Let him be happy like us.

The blessings we experience on these happy shores

Our hearts are not jealous.

He sees them, let him share them,

Let him be happy like us.

(Various Quadrilles of Shades approach Castor.)

A FEMALE SHADE:

Over fugitive shades

Love still casts his flames,

But on these shores

He only makes happy lovers.

(With carefree dances the shades express their differing characters.)

A FEMALE SHADE:

(alternatively with the Chorus)

In these sweet asylums

Your wishes will be crowned.

Come,

These charming climes

Are destined to peaceful pleasures.

This enchanted stream,

Happy Lethe

Flows here amongst the flowers

Where one sees neither sorrows

Nor cares, nor longings

Nor tears.

Forgetfulness brings with it

Neither cares nor boredom.

This god leaves us

Without ending

The memory

Of pleasure.

(The Shades resume their dances; suddenly they are interrupted.)

CHORUS:

(Off stage) Flee, flee, flighty shades,

Our sports are being profaned by bold eyes.

(Pollux appears and the astonished shades flee before him.)

POLLUX:

Relax, fortunate dwellers

In this favorable asylum far away from trouble.

I'm coming to experience the peace that you give.

It's here that heroes dwell in tranquility.

Dear Shade appear—

CASTOR:

(noticing Pollux) O my brother! Is it you?

O moments of tenderness!

TOGETHER:

O most sweet moments!

O my brother! Is this you?

POLLUX:

It's I, coming to break the chain that binds you;

It's I, who avenged you on an odious rival.

CASTOR:

I will see the light of the Heavens?

POLLUX:

It's very little to give you back life.

Fate is raising you to the rank of the gods.

CASTOR:

What do I hear? What happiness! I will leave these climes.

And Heaven will permit me to live near you?

POLLUX:

No, you will enjoy alone a sweet portion,

And jealous destiny

Is going to impose on me

The fetters from which my hand is delivering you.

CASTOR:

I shall purchase life through your death, o Heaven!

POLLUX:

The entire universe demands your return,

Reign over a faithful people.

CASTOR:

The son of Jupiter must rule.

POLLUX:

See in the Heavens the glory that's calling you.

CASTOR:

I am sacrificing all immortal grandeur

To the sole pleasure which approaches me from you.

POLLUX:

Telaire is awaiting you.

CASTOR:

Spare me, cruel one;

She herself would look with terror at this price,

The criminal plot to renew my life.

POLLUX:

Castor, we will ruin the two of us.

If you keep delaying you will cost her her life.

Hasten, go, Heaven orders you to be happy,

And it's your rival that begs you.

CASTOR:

Yes, in the end I am giving in to your prayers.

I will go to save the life of a faithful lover,

I will be born again for her;

But since, at last, I am reaching the rank of the Immortals

I swear by the Styx that a second dawn

Will not find me in the abode of mortals.

I only want to see her and adore her again,

And then I will return you to life, your throne, and your altars.

POLLUX:

(to Mercury) His life's going to begin.

Fly, Mercury, obey,

Take an Immortal to the abode of thunder,

A hero to earth.

Fly, Mercury, obey.

CHORUS OF SHADES:

Return, return to somber shores,

Both of you, dwell amongst us.

And we will make the gods jealous

Of the happiness of Shades.

(Mercury carries off Castor in a cloud; Pollux extends his arm to him and withdraws with the happy Shades.)

CURTAIN

ACT V
SCENE 7

The stage represents an agreeable view in the environs of Sparta.

TELAIRE:

Heaven is then touched by the most tender loves;

Your voice recalls me to life that I was leaving.

You will live, to be faithful to me,

And you will live forever.

CASTOR:

Alas!

TELAIRE:

But why these alarms?

You love me, I see you—

CASTOR:

Telaire, live.

TELAIRE:

What am I hearing? What speech?

CASTOR:

Telaire?

TELAIRE:

Get to the point;

Is the most beautiful day of our life made for tears?

CASTOR:

We must prepare for eternal farewells.

TELAIRE:

What are you saying? O Heaven!

CASTOR:

We must separate,

I am returning to somber shores.

TELAIRE:

Castor! And you will abandon me!

CASTOR:

My brother and my oaths are awaiting me at the home of Shades.

TELAIRE:

My eyes are condemned to weep for you again!

Hardly do I see you! Hardly do I breathe!

Castor! And you will abandon me!

CASTOR:

The fatal moment is approaching,

It hurries me, it is expiring.

What a moment of horrors and attraction this is!

TELAIRE:

Alas! Can I believe you?

Ingrate, you are glorying in such a perjury to Love

To be faithful to death. (songs of rejoicing are heard)

But I hear shouts of joy.

(A troupe of Spartans enters and comes before Castor.)

CHORUS:

Live, happy spouses.

TELAIRE:

All these people are rushing before your steps.

Do you intend to trouble their sports? They were prepared for us.

CASTOR:

(to the people)

Alas! You are unaware that your expectation is vain.

TELAIRE AND CHORUS:

Why do you rob us of such sweet distractions?

CASTOR:

Folks, distance yourselves.

Your wishes increase my pain.

(The people leave.)

TELAIRE:

Eh! What! All these objects cannot soften you?

CASTOR:

Do you want me to abandon my brother to Hell?

TELAIRE:

The gods will return him to us; Jupiter is his father.

CASTOR:

Live and let me die.

TELAIRE:

You die!

Then for whom do you expect that I will continue to breathe?

CASTOR:

Reign! My brother is immortal;

My brother adores you.

TELAIRE:

No, I will not await such a cruel destiny.

I will shall call the gods to witness the death that I implore.

CASTOR:

Stop, beware the charm of your tears.

If I dared to hesitate, it is because of vengeful gods,

They perhaps will punish my passion on you and on me.

TELAIRE:

With what new horror are you coming to strike my soul?

CASTOR:

I would antagonize Jupiter, his son has my oaths.

TELAIRE:

They've loved, these gods, they will pity lovers. (the sound of several thunderbolts is heard)

What did I hear! What uproar! What flashes of lightning!

Alas! It's I who ruined you.

CASTOR:

I hear the air quiver! I feel the earth tremble!

It's all over! I've waited too long.

TOGETHER:

Halt, vengeful god, halt.

(The uproar increases.)

CASTOR:

Hell is opening beneath my feet!

Thunder growls over my head! (Telaire falls fainting from terror)

Heaven! O Heaven! Telaire's expiring in my arms!

Halt, vengeful god, halt! (a melodious symphony succeeds the thunderous uproar)

But the roaring is stopping—open your eyes,

Nature is sensitive to out torments

And these harmonious concerts

Are announcing a more peaceable god.

(Jupiter descends from Heaven on his eagle.)

JUPITER:

The Fates are satisfied: your fate is halted;

I free you forever from the oath which entangled you.

You will no longer see the shore

That your brother has already left.

He lives, and Jupiter permits you to share

In immortality.

(Pollux appears.)

CASTOR:

My brother! O Heaven!

POLLUX:

Gods! I find together

All the objects of my love!

CASTOR:

I was going to deliver you from those dark climes

When Heaven, at last, rejoined us.

CASTOR AND TELAIRE:

Gods, who are creating for us

A fate so full of attraction,

O gods! Don't separate us.

POLLUX:

Hell shall have only one victim.

I saw Phoebe descend to the shores of death,

An unfortunate love precipitated her steps,

And love made her entire crime.

JUPITER:

Palace of my grandeur, where I dictate my laws,

Vast empire of gods, open to my voice.

SCENE BREAK

ACT V
SCENE 8

The Heavens open and reveal on all sides of the stage the pavilions which serve the principal celestial divinities, born by clouds. In the rear is the palace of Jupiter, formed by a transparent colonnade through which is visible in the distance a part of the Zodiac with the sign of the Twins where they are installed. The sun is on its chariot, pursuing its course. All the heavenly divinities are gathered, as well as the Genies who preside over the planets.

All the gods of Olympus, the Celestial Genies, the Hours, etc. appear.

JUPITER:

(to Castor and Pollux) So many virtues must pretend

To a share of our altars.

Let's offer to the universe immortal signs

Of a friendship so pure and a love so tender.

ALL THE CHORUSES:

Let the heavens, the earth and the oceans

Shine with a thousand diverse flames.

It's the order of the master of the world,

It's the fest of the universe.

(Ballets showing the Hours and the Planets.)

CASTOR:

How sweet it is to wear your chains!

Tender love, your pleasures make your sorrows forgotten.

I've made your flames shine in a hundred different climes

To show the entire Universe

How sweet it is to wear your chains.

They all told me in Hell

That it's sweet to bear your chains,

And when the heavens opened for me

I heard echo in the air

That it's sweet to wear your chains.

(The Chorus blends its voice with Castor's and repeats the last verse.)

CHORUS:

Let the heavens, the earth and the ocean

Shine with a thousand diverse flames.

It's the order of the master of the world,

It's the fest of the universe.

CURTAIN

PENELOPE
BY JEAN-FRANÇOIS MARMONTEL,
Music by Niccolò Piccinni

CAST OF CHARACTERS

PENELOPE, wife of Ulysses

NESUS

THEONE

EUMAEUS

TELEMACHUS, son of Ulysses

LAERTES, father of Ulysses

ULYSSES

SHEPHERD

NYMPH

CHORUS—of Suitors, of Women, of Deputies, of Nymphs, of the People of Ithaca

ACT I
SCENE 1

The stage represents the vestibule of the Palace of Ulysses, and before it a hall where Penelope's suitors are dining.

CHORUS OF SUITORS:

(at the back)

Let's leave the lovers of glory

To seek death or victory

In the most distant climes.

Amongst games and feasts,

A most sweet passion urges us.

God of love, god of intoxication,

You preside over our destinies.

PENELOPE:

(at the front of the stage, hearing them)

What's increasing their barbarous mirth today?

Have they most certain information about my misfortune?

CHORUS OF SUITORS:

God of love, god of intoxication,

You preside over our destinies.

PENELOPE:

Vile and cowardly tyrants, the opprobrium of Greece!

CHORUS:

God of love, etc.

PENELOPE:

They ceaselessly swim in joy.

And as for me, in sorrow, I feel myself extinguished.

CHORUS:

Among games and feasts

God of love, god of intoxication,

You preside over our destinies.

(Enter The Deputies of the People.)

THE DEPUTIES:

(to Penelope) A people, overwhelmed with sadness,

Sighing, extends hands to you.

Do you intend for us to lament forever

Under inhuman oppressors?

PENELOPE:

(aside) Enslaved people, it's your weakness

Which makes the ills for which I am pitying myself.

DEPUTIES:

Give in to the wishes we addresses to you.

Our destinies depend on you.

PENELOPE:

Enslaved people, it's your weakness

Which makes the ills for which I am pitying myself.

SUITORS:

God of love, god of intoxication,

You are presiding over our destinies.

(The Suitors withdraw.)

PENELOPE:

(to the Deputies)

I know your misfortunes, and my courage shares them.

If I have no further hope, if my spouse is dead,

They want me to entangle myself in a new marriage.

On the return of my son, I will submit to my fate.

Don't ask for more.

(The Deputies withdraw.)

PENELOPE:

Just gods, avenging gods, are you abandoning us?

Ah! Return to me my son, return my spouse to me.

(Air)

Captive Queen,

Fearful mother,

Spouse in tears,

To what misfortunes

Heaven is delivering me!

Cease, cruel ones, to pursue me

Or I will succumb to my sorrows.

Return my son, return,

Your perils are mine.

If you perish on the ocean

Who will be my support?

Return to your mother the only blessing

That still remains to her in the world.

Return, my son, return,

Your perils are mine.

(Nesus and his followers enter.)

NESUS:

Tremble, Queen, tremble that your wish is accomplished.

The snare of death awaits the son of Ulysses.

If he returns, if he lands, he will perish under the waves.

PENELOPE:

Telemachus!

NESUS:

Witness the darkest conspiracies.

I didn't want to be an accomplice to it

And I am waiting only for a propitious wind

To sail to Delos.

PENELOPE:

You let Telemachus perish.

THEONE:

You, the only one of twenty kings who make Ithaca shake,

The only one from whom Penelope expected help!

NESUS:

I was going to shorten the course of her calamities.

Everything has changed. Her heart refuses itself to my wishes,

Her delays, her evasions are very well known to me.

I no longer wish to nourish a hope that abuses me.

Of whatever wrong she accuses me of,

Let her accuse her scorn.

THEONE:

What love!

NESUS:

In a generous and sincere heart,

Deceived love changes into a mortal scorn.

But if it's in me that she hopes

To give to Telemachus a defender, a father,

She has only to wish it:

I am waiting for her at the altar.

(He leaves.)

PENELOPE:

O crime, o detestable wickedness!

In this shocking peril,

What to decide? To whom to turn?

My son, I am reduced to the inevitable choice

Of betraying my spouse or seeing you perish.

CHORUS OF WOMEN:

O unhappy mother!

Your son's going to perish.

PENELOPE:

O unhappy mother!

To what god to turn?

Alas! If I delay,

My son, you are going to die.

Must I betray your father?

Must I see you perish?

CHORUS OF WOMEN:

O unhappy mother!

Your son's going to perish.

PENELOPE:

O unhappy mother!

To what god to turn?

There remains one hope to me; it's that a favorable wind,

Or rather a favorable god,

Is opposing his return and keeping him away from port.

Alas! To what is fate reducing me!

This return, this moment so desirable to me,

Terrifies me more than death.

(Eumaeus enters.)

THEONE:

Eumaeus, what brings you around here?

EUMAEUS:

Heaven is touched by our tears,

Telemachus is coming back.

PENELOPE:

God!

EUMAEUS:

On the moist plain

I have recognized the colors of his pavilions.

PENELOPE:

O funereal day!—I am dying. (she falls into the arms of her women)

THEONE:

Go, wise and faithful friend,

With a swift ship beg for help,

Keep Telemachus away; they are after his life.

EUMAEUS:

His life is threatened!

THEONE:

In her mortal terror,

The Queen has only you to turn to.

EUMAEUS:

Alas! What can my zeal do for him,

In such a great peril and with time so short!

(Eumaeus leaves.)

PENELOPE:

(in fright and distress)

It's over with. Death surrounds him.

Today, Nesus alone could

Save him, defend him, and Nesus is abandoning him!

Ah! If there's still time, go, my darling Theone,

Implore his support,

Let him deliver my son, let him return him to his mother.

That's enough; for the reward of a head so dear

I engage myself, or rather, I abandon myself to him.

(Theone leaves.)

CHORUS:

From the breast of the saddest alarms

See beautiful days reborn.

Hymen, escorted by Cherubs,

Will soon have dried your tears.

From the breast of the saddest alarms

See beautiful days reborn.

(During this chorus Penelope remains absorbed in her sorrow.)

PENELOPE:

What have I promised? Ah! Unfortunate woman!

Either my spouse is breathing or his shade hears me

From the breast of dark night,

Between the altar and myself, I see who's awaiting me there.

(air)

Yes, there I see, this wandering shade.

It's himself; yes, I see it.

He's plaintive and shivering.

He's terrible and threatening.

Dear shade, approach, appease yourself.

I swore to you to be forever faithful

And for my eternal constancy

I take all the gods for witness.

But if I am not criminal

Your son is going to perish before my eyes.

(The Suitors enter.)

PENELOPE:

Which of you, which of you, perfidious ones,

Is getting ready to strike me in my breast?

Stained with the blood of my son, of which you are avid,

Who will be the assassin of his mother today?

CHORUS OF SUITORS:

Who can impute this guilty plan to us?

PENELOPE:

Yes, sacrilegious one that you are,

Yes, you've conceived this odious crime

In the breast of your barbarous feasts,

In the palace of Ulysses, in the face of the gods.

CHORUS:

The mortal terror

That reigns in your soul

Can instantly calm itself at the altar.

Between twenty kings,

Enflamed by the same ardor,

Make a choice.

Your wishes will be our law.

PENELOPE:

(excitedly)

Let my son be returned to me, let him announce it to me himself,

That Ulysses has descended to the night of the tomb.

Henceforth, to protect him, I renounce my word

And I am going to relight the torch of Hymen.

CHORUS OF SUITORS:

No, no, it's a trick.

It's a new subterfuge.

PENELOPE:

Alas, yet another day.

CHORUS OF SUITORS:

No, no, it's another trick.

PENELOPE:

O mortal constraint!

CHORUS OF SUITORS:

It's a new subterfuge.

PENELOPE:

You are freezing me with fear.

CHORUS OF SUITORS:

Surrender, surrender without fear

To this most ardent love.

PENELOPE:

You freeze me with fear

And you speak of love!

CHORUS:

Surrender, etc.

PENELOPE:

Is it necessary to complete my misery,

To deliver to you my estates, my palace, my treasures;

That a ship instantly distance me from these shores?

I will go to Icarus, my father,

To forget all the treasure you have ravished me of.

Only with me let me take my son.

That's a mother's only treasure.

CHORUS OF SUITORS:

Name the spouse that your heart prefers.

And in an instant your tears are going to dry up.

CHORUS OF WOMEN:

O unhappy mother!

Your son is going to perish.

PENELOPE:

O unhappy mother!

It's for me to die. (A symphonic movement announces the arrival of Telemachus)

God! My son!

(Telemachus enters with Eumaeus and the People. Penelope throws herself into his arms.)

TELEMACHUS:

At last, august Queen,

Our misfortunes are going to finish:

Ulysses is not far away.

PENELOPE:

He is living.

TELEMACHUS:

Heaven is just

And it has taken care of the life of a hero itself. (air)

Covered with the immortal shield

He's going to return to his estates.

Insult, injury, and cruelty

Are going to see their attempts punished.

In terror and silence

Let all abase themselves before him

Far from us, guilty license.

Reassure yourself, weak innocence,

The gods are returning you their support.

CHORUS OF SUITORS:

(aside) Imprudent youth, your hope

Will be confounded today.

PENELOPE:

Gods, protectors of innocence,

You are declaring yourselves today.

CHORUS OF PEOPLE:

To the sweet rays of hope

Our hearts are open today.

TELEMACHUS:

Reassure yourself, weak innocence,

The gods are returning you their support.

CHORUS OF SUITORS:

Imprudent youth, your hope

Will be confounded today.

CURTAIN

ACT II
SCENE 2

The stage represents a hamlet where one makes out the old castle of Laertes and the house of Eumaeus. The sea can be seen in the distance.

EUMAEUS:

Cease, venerable Laertes,

Cease to lament for the loss

Of a son so long awaited.

He breathes, he's coming back.

LAERTES:

Have I really heard it?

Before leaving the light

I will embrace my son! Then it's enough, great gods.

I will join my ancestors without regret amongst the dead

If the hand of my son shuts my eye.

How many ills his absence has caused hereabouts.

But who has just announced the news of his return

To his faithful spouse?

TELEMACHUS:

(entering) I, Lord.

LAERTES:

Heaven! What do I see? Shall I believe my own eyes?

Dear Prince, object of my tenderness,

Is it you that I am pressing in my weak arms?

How many perils I see you've escaped! (excitedly)

Do you have confidence of the return of my son?

A very insubstantial hope

Hasn't deceived you?

TELEMACHUS:

He's returning. Gods and men

All conspire to assure me of it.

LAERTES:

(sad and tender) Let him come without delay.

Alas! In the condition we are in

I no longer have the time to hope

(air)

In my languishing old age

I see the torch going out.

I'm touching the edge of my tomb

And for me no long wait.

O death: slow down a bit

Leave me a day so fine.

(A crowd of Shepherds enters.)

LAERTES:

(excitedly) Come, herdsmen, come congratulate a father.

I will console myself for twenty years of misfortunes.

Heaven's returning a son to me; it wants what I am hoping for.

A SHEPHERD:

The rumor of his return has flown to us.

CHORUS AND TELEMACHUS:

Adored Prince, what gaiety

You are pouring into all hearts.

Ulysses was seen in Greece;

And you are awaiting him on these shores!

LAERTES WITH THE CHORUS:

To their love, to my tenderness,

To our love, to his tenderness,

Beneficent gods, are returning him to you

(The shepherds express their joy through dances. The music announces the approach of a storm. The stage darkens.)

EUMAEUS:

(to Telemachus) Prince, you can observe from the shore

A boat beaten by the waves

And the terror of sailors

Is announcing a violent storm.

(The music expresses the progress of the storm.)

CHORUS:

What uproar in the air!

The waves are replying to it!

The heavens and the seas

Already are confounding themselves.

On the foaming ocean,

Gods! What tortures!

What somber horror!

To the roar of thunder

The winds in fury

Are giving themselves to war.

Heaven is spreading

Terror on earth.

TELEMACHUS:

How I pity the fate

Of so many victims.

EUMAEUS:

Immense abysses

Are offering them death.

TELEMACHUS:

O gods! If my father

Were running this danger!

LAERTES:

O god! If your father

Were running this danger!

EUMAEUS:

O gods! If his father

Were running this danger.

THE THREE:

Neptune in wrath

Is going to submerge them.

CHORUS AND THE THREE:

What lamentable screams!

What funereal uproar!

The unconquerable billow

Is breaking them and vanishing.

(All withdraw.)

BLACKOUT

ACT II
SCENE 3

The scene represents the grotto of the sea Nymphs.

ULYSSES:

(alone) All perished. On to what shore

Are the furious winds hurling me?

Alone, distracted, unarmed, amongst a savage nation,

Am I going to find death or slavery here?

What do I see? Shall I believe my eyes?

Everything reminds me of Ithaca.

Yes, this beautiful place resembles

That beautiful grotto, where on our shores

The chorus of nymphs assembled

And made the air echo with its divine harmonies.

(Ulysses withdraws at the approach of the Nymphs.)

(Enter the Sea Nymphs.)

CHORUS OF NYMPHS:

Day is reborn, the winds are quieting down,

A more serene heaven is smiling upon us.

The air has calmed, the waves are appeased;

On the shore everything is flourishing.

Timid pleasures, reappear,

That terror has dispersed.

Come, tender love, you who guide them,

Come, revive their hearts like the terror that froze them.

(Ulysses reenters.)

ULYSSES:

O Nymphs, reassure my timid presence.

Alas! If I believe in the appearance,

I've burned incense for you here a hundred times

A NYMPH:

And who doesn't know the shores to which you are descending!

The name of Ithaca and its glory

Are borne by victory

Unto the farthest climes.

ULYSSES:

Beautiful nymph, is it true? You are not flattering me?

And am I, indeed, in Ithaca?

Laertes, Penelope, and her son Telemachus,

Are they living? Are they peacefully united?

NYMPH:

Violence and injustice

Threaten mother and son.

CHORUS OF NYMPHS:

Go see them again, prudent Ulysses,

Dissimulate, observe, and punish.

NYMPH:

Minerva, has imprinted old age on your face

To deceive the eyes of your court.

CHORUS:

Arm yourself with a fearless heart

And, especially, defend yourself against tears of love.

(The Nymphs leave.)

ULYSSES:

(alone) What misfortune is again predicted to me?

Haven't I suffered enough?

Penelope, o you that I adore!

And you my son, at your dawn,

Far from me, what abyss has opened beneath your feet?

What misfortune is again predicted to me?

Haven't I suffered enough?

Ithaca! O my sweet homeland!

I've sighed only for you.

I've seen you again, cherished isle,

And I cannot see you without terror!

I escaped the sea in its fury,

Calm is finally reborn in me;

I've seen you again, cherished isle,

And I cannot see you without terror.

What misfortune, etc.

Who's coming to me in this shore?

(Enter Telemachus and Eumaeus.)

TELEMACHUS:

Worthy stranger, wasn't it you

That we saw hurled on this shore by a shipwreck?

Ah! It was some god who rescued you

From that horrible danger.

ULYSSES:

Yes, young man, yes, this prodigy is the work of the gods;

And as unfortunate as I am

I experience the blessings as much as I can.

TELEMACHUS:

Hasten to calm our mortal fears

In this ship broken by the winds in their wrath.

A hero, the object of our tears,

Ulysses, was he with you?

ULYSSES:

I know he was voyaging towards Ithaca.

TELEMACHUS:

Did the gods separate him?

ULYSSES:

Then it's here that he reigned?

TELEMACHUS:

You see his son Telemachus.

You see his faithful friend.

ULYSSES:

You, his son!

TELEMACHUS:

Ah! speak. Your heart shook.

ULYSSES:

Alas! what mortal stain

I bring to your sensitive hearts.

Will your mother survive it?

He is—

TELEMACHUS:

Don't finish. I see all our misfortunes.

EUMAEUS:

Then it's true! The gods have ended his life.

TELEMACHUS:

All hope is ravished from me.

My too weak youth was expecting everything from him;

And amongst the dangers with which it is pursued,

Here I am henceforth without guide and without support!

ULYSSES:

(aside) Delightful moment! Joy worthy of being envied!

EUMAEUS:

Eh! What! The last one of his ships

Which had defied the rage of winds and seas

Has just broken up on this shore

And my unfortunate Master perished under the waves!

ULYSSES:

He saw the shipwreck without weakness and without fear

And braved death with an intrepid eye.

But, alas! What can courage do

Against the order of the gods and the decrees of fate.

TELEMACHUS:

O my father!

EUMAEUS:

O my master!

TELEMACHUS:

Cruel fate!

EUMAEUS:

Frightful day!

EUMAEUS AND TELEMACHUS:

(together)

Who will be happy?

Ulysses couldn't be.

ULYSSES:

(aside) Ah! what father, ah! What master

Was ever more lucky!

TELEMACHUS:

I've lost my model,

I've lost my support.

EUMAEUS:

His faithful spouse

Was living only for him.

ULYSSES:

What happiness, today

She was expecting him by her!

TELEMACHUS AND EUMAEUS:

He no longer exists for her.

She can no longer exist without him.

ULYSSES:

He is happy still

If he's living in all hearts.

TELEMACHUS AND EUMAEUS:

If he's living in all hearts!

And you, you still doubt it,

You, seeing our tears?

He's a god one adores.

ULYSSES:

(aside) I feel my tears pouring out.

EUMAEUS:

How to offer ourselves

To the eyes of the Queen?

TELEMACHUS:

O gods! What pain

Her heart is going to suffer!

TOGETHER:

Very faithful witness

Of our misfortune,

From pity for her,

Deceive her sorrow.

ULYSSES:

(aside) My soul staggers;

A troublesome conqueror

Distracts me and is betraying

The depths of my heart. (end of trio)

Open your eyes, my dear Eumaeus.

EUMAEUS:

What am I hearing? My soul was accustomed to that voice.

Telemachus! O beneficent gods!

Why, no, it's not him: this extreme age,

These hairs whitened by the years—

ULYSSES:

It's him; it's Ulysses himself.

TELEMACHUS:

(struck with astonishment and distracted by joy)

My father!

ULYSSES:

In vain, Minerva wanted to hide me

Under all the features of age.

Come, recognize your father in the tender tears

That love and joy are tearing from me.

TELEMACHUS:

(in the arms of Ulysses)

Father! Finally, I see the author of my being.

ULYSSES:

Let's moderate these distractions, and keep silent

Before announcing my return.

My uneasy vigilance

Intends to observe everything in my court.

EUMAEUS:

Ah! Beware the violence of our proud tyrants.

ULYSSES:

Your tyrants!

EUMAEUS:

Oppressed Ithaca laments

Under twenty kings, your unworthy rivals.

Penelope, consumed by troubles and trembling,

Sees them delivered endlessly to a thousand new excesses.

ULYSSES:

(aside) Ah! Let my hand be armed with my vengeful darts

And I am going to crown my labors with their death.

My son, danger is surrounding me.

What will you do for me?

TELEMACHUS:

(excitedly) Command. By your side,

Father, a thousand deaths would not astound me.

I witness the gods and the blood from which I come.

ULYSSES:

If we are loved, we will be very strong.

The rumor of my death, that we are going to spread,

These white hairs, these features that Minerva has distorted,

These kings whose imprudence is easy to surprise,

My son, all answer to me, that we will be avenged.

(air)

May vengeance march slowly

Under an impenetrable veil.

You shall perish, execrable troupe

And all my blows will be bloody.

We won't show to your insolent eyes

Anything but a weak and miserable old geezer.

May vengeance march slowly

Under an impenetrable veil.

ULYSSES, TELEMACHUS AND EUMAEUS:

Let vengeance march slowly

Under an impenetrable veil.

You shall perish, execrable troupe,

And all our blows will be bloody.

CURTAIN

ACT III
SCENE 4

The stage represents a room in the Palace of Ulysses.

ULYSSES:

Is she finally going to appear?

TELEMACHUS:

She's coming on my heels.

ULYSSES:

I want to be alone with her.

Leave us alone and spread the news

Of my death.

TELEMACHUS:

You are going to tear apart her tender, faithful heart.

ULYSSES:

Obey, my son, and don't hesitate.

(Telemachus leaves.)

ULYSSES:

(alone) What haven't I suffered, to see her in silence

Endure the humiliating ostentation of these kings?

What haven't I suffered, to see their insolence

Insult the misfortune of a suppliant old geezer?

(air)

Ah! How painful is prudence

Between wrath and love,

What torment for a heart to choke, turn by turn,

A burning rage, a pitiful sensibility!

Twenty times my eyes covered themselves

As with a cloud of tears.

And twenty times I shook not to have my weapons

To exterminate these perverts.

Don't go forgetting the advice of Minerva,

Ulysses! They're listening to you, they're observing you.

Here's the moment to employ

The great art of dissimulation.

Command your looks, compose your face,

Forbid your tears to shed.

Here she is! What a moment! And what am I going to tell her?

(Enter Penelope and women in her following.)

PENELOPE:

Come closer, I respect age and its misfortune.

You see us in sorrow

But our ills are going to end, since Ulysses is breathing.

Then he's left Corcyra?

You saw him?

ULYSSES:

I said the simple truth.

PENELOPE:

Didn't you learn from his mouth

What interests him and what touches me?

ULYSSES:

I know that he suffered harsh adversity;

I know that far from his country,

Cast from peril to peril for a long while

In the horror of battles, on infuriated seas,

Your cherished image

Never left him for a single moment.

PENELOPE:

Ah! How guilty I would be,

If, far from him, my heart had been capable

Of a moment of tranquility.

(air)

Since the moment of our parting

I haven't ceased to see Ulysses,

And for my torture, his dangers

Are all present to my eyes.

Wind, water, sword, flame,

All that can threaten a mortal's life,

Bring terror to my heart.

Sometimes I hoped, but always, I was afraid.

ULYSSES:

The more painful glory is, the greater its charms.

Sometimes Ulysses enjoyed it.

On the tomb of Achilles, in the midst of twenty kings,

He battled for the arms of Achilles against proud Ajax.

PENELOPE:

And as soon as they heard his eloquent voice

He doubtless triumphed.

ULYSSES:

He made tears flow

And softened hearts recognized his rights.

PENELOPE:

You don't astonish me. My Ulysses possesses

In the art of persuasion a charm that all surrender to.

ULYSSES:

Under the walls of Ilion, now covered with ashes,

Companion of heroes, he won their esteem.

But new dangers were awaiting him at sea

He saw the frightful abyss of Scylla and Charybdis.

PENELOPE:

O gods!

ULYSSES:

The roaring waves bore him on their peaks

Between two open gulfs.

PENELOPE:

Ah! His past perils make me shiver once more.

ULYSSES:

Circë, who could dim day that

Her father the Sun god caused to bloom,

Saw Ulysses in danger and deigned to welcome him.

PENELOPE:

Circë!

ULYSSES:

Through a sweet intoxication

The perfidious woman tried to obscure his reason

But Ulysses avoided the poison

Of the enchantress's cup.

PENELOPE:

(air)

You knew how much my tenderness

Must wish for your return,

My dear Ulysses! And wisdom

Will preserve you less than love.

ULYSSES:

More sincere, and more dangerous, Calypso,

In her happy isle,

Invited your spouse to immortality.

PENELOPE:

Ah! How to resist the charms of a loving woman

Who proposes such a reward for infidelity!

ULYSSES:

A charming Nymph, a bewitching abode,

The fate of gods, Ulysses left them all for you.

PENELOPE:

It's my happiness to believe it.

Doubt was too cruel.

No, no, he hasn't lost

The memory of a mutual love.

No, the wisest of mortals

Will not have betrayed the altars,

His faith, my love, and his glory.

It's my happiness to believe him

The most faithful of mortals.

(Enter the Suitors, Eumaeus, Nesus.)

NESUS:

Finally, the funereal fate of Ulysses

Is no longer doubtful; he's descended to the home of the dead.

PENELOPE:

What are you daring to say?

SUITOR:

He just perished on these shores.

And it's this stranger who attests to it.

PENELOPE:

Him!

ULYSSES:

(to Nesus) Cruelty! Ah! Why dispel her error.

PENELOPE:

Ulysses is dead!

ULYSSES:

I fled the deplorable remains

Of his ship, broken by the winds in their fury.

PENELOPE:

Old Geezer, they've probably enticed you to overwhelm me.

Already, to humor these kings,

Strangers more than once

Have used the same language.

Man, in misfortune, is so weak at your age

And over him fear and hope

Sometimes have too much power!

Intimidated, seduced by these kings, perhaps

Without knowing him, you are conspiring.

Ah! You don't know what heart you are tearing apart.

If it's only a mistake, let me know it.

There is still time, yet. But life, or my death,

Depends on you, don't doubt it.

A word, a single word decides it.

I see you are softening; you seem to me to be hiding from me

The horror that inspires in you a perfidious plot.

You pity it, this heart that they want to snatch from me.

From pity of my life that you are going to shorten,

Speak. Here, where the majesty of gods resides:

You are running no danger under their eyes.

Be sincere in confidence.

Is Ulysses living? My sickly hope,

Should it revive or die?

ULYSSES:

(low) O gods! Sustain my courage.

(aloud) Queen, you are insulting my humility.

PENELOPE:

Good old man, pardon, I am doing you an outrage;

Yet, I admit it, a confused movement

Is obstinately rising against you in my heart.

I am questioning your eyes, your features, your language,

Everything there depicts candor to me. Well, at this moment

I don't know what voice in secret gives you the lie.

For me, perhaps, it's a weak omen!

But alarmed a hundred times, and always in vain,

What proof urges me to believe you today?

ULYSSES:

Alas! How vain your suspicions

And how really easy it is to elucidate this cloud!

Queen, on your fidelity, recognize the token

That Ulysses left in my hand.

PENELOPE:

The ring of Ulysses! O gods! O pitiless fate!

I can no longer doubt my misfortune.

ULYSSES:

Ah! Think how much it cost me

To announce this terrifying misfortune to you.

PENELOPE:

(air)

He is horrible, he is evil,

He didn't know about my heart.

Who never loved like I love

Cannot conceive my misfortune.

So long as the weakest semblance

Could flatter me in my suffering

Life had appeal for me;

But a misfortune without hope

Is only a long and painful death

He is horrible, etc.

TELEMACHUS:

Gods! She's succumbing. My mother! (holding her in his arms and looking at Ulysses)

Is there no more to be hoped?

PENELOPE:

What do you want me to hope?

He saw his shipwreck, and you heard him.

No, I no longer have a spouse, no, you no longer have a father.

My son, we've lost everything.

O heaven! This is the share of virtue!

After all the dangers he just ran,

He came to perish on the shores that saw his birth.

Go, Eumaeus, go, search the shore

And among the debris rejected by the waves

Gather on the beach

The sacred remains of a hero.

At least let my sorrow ease itself by honoring him. (Eumaeus leaves)

You, my son, let a tomb be raised to his shade.

It will be drenched every day by my tears.

ULYSSES:

Prince, don't forget to hang his arms on it.

PENELOPE:

Alas! It's a fine enough trophy for his glory. (to Suitors)

And you who are rejoicing in the misfortune that overwhelms me,

Since, in the end, heaven is implacable,

Forcing me to renounce these fetters so dear to me

At the foot of this tomb that my people are erecting,

It's there that I intend that they hear

What I have promised to announce.

CHORUS OF SUITORS:

Queen, fate is commanding you:

There's no longer time to hesitate.

(The Suitors withdraw.)

ULYSSES:

What have you decided?

PENELOPE:

My death; I am reduced to it,

It's my only hope and I intend to have recourse to it.

CHORUS OF WOMEN:

O gods! You're a mother and you intend to die!

PENELOPE:

I intend to free myself from a frightful pursuit.

ULYSSES:

A son still remains to you: he can aid you.

PENELOPE:

Alas! They are threatening him in the arms of his mother.

ULYSSES:

They are threatening him!

PENELOPE:

And it's for him

That they made me tremble today.

ULYSSES:

(in an imposing tone)

Heaven is at last ridding itself of these no-goods

You will see your tyrants fall.

PENELOPE:

(astonished) And what god will accomplish this miracle?

ULYSSES:

(in an inspired tone)

Ulysses predicted it: trust in this oracle;

The future unveils itself to the eyes of the dying.

Live, Queen, live; he himself orders it.

Yes, I am coming to reveal his supreme will.

It will make your odious tyrants tremble.

PENELOPE:

Ah! What unknown trouble your are tossing into my soul!

Under the features of a mortal, are you one of the gods?

ULYSSES:

Mortal though I be, I predict that before your eyes,

Like a flaming arrow, the vengeance of heaven

Is soon going to arrive.

PENELOPE:

Yes, it's some god who is inspiring him.

I can no longer doubt it.

ULYSSES:

Follow me then without hesitation,

And this I dare to predict to you,

Come see it executed.

(They leave together.)

CURTAIN

ACT III
SCENE 5

The stage represents a public square; the tomb of Ulysses in the middle of it. Telemachus is present.

CHORUS OF THE PEOPLE OF ITHACA:

Let's weep for the wisest of kings.

The world is full of his glory.

We will no longer live under his laws.

Of his virtues, of his exploits

Let's preserve the memory forever.

We will no longer live under his laws.

(Enter Penelope, Ulysses, and the Suitors.)

PENELOPE:

Son of Ulysses, and you people, a venerable old man,

Witness to his deplorable fate,

Comes to bring our hearts the most sensitive blows.

He says, he received Ulysses' supreme will

Which he's coming to announce to me before you.

There's nothing under heaven more sacred for us.

But I intend for him to attest to it, with an oath right there

On the tomb of my spouse.

ULYSSES:

(after having mounted the steps of the tomb on which he rests his hand)

Yes, I attest to the death of inflexible tyrants,

On the tomb of Ulysses and his terrible armor,

That he was unable without shaking to know you were in danger,

That he pitied your misfortunes,

And that he's coming to avenge them.

PENELOPE, THE SUITORS, THE PEOPLE:

Heaven!

ULYSSES:

(to the Suitors) Tremble, wretches, recognize Ulysses!

GENERAL CHORUS:

Ulysses! O gods!

ULYSSES:

(to his son and to the people of Ithaca)

For their death,

Take arms, take arms.

(He distributes weapons to them.)

CHORUS OF PEOPLE AND SUITORS:

Let's arm ourselves, let's arm ourselves.

(The Suitors distance themselves; Ulysses and his partisans cross the stage and leave the same, following the suitors.)

PENELOPE:

Ah! The excess of my joy overcomes my weakness.

CHORUS WITH PENELOPE:

It's him! It's Ulysses! Great gods!

CHORUS OF PEOPLE OFF STAGE:

Fall, audacious tyrants!

PENELOPE:

Alas! In what worry he's leaving me!

CHORUS ON STAGE:

Protect us, wise goddess,

Ulysses is fighting before your eyes.

CHORUS OFF STAGE:

Fall, audacious tyrants.

SUITORS:

Let's flee the danger that's rushing on us.

Ulysses has all the gods for him.

CHORUS OFF STAGE:

Fall under his vengeful hand,

Fall, audacious tyrants.

CHORUS ON STAGE:

Protect us, wise goddess!

Ulysses is fighting before your eyes.

PENELOPE:

(rushing to Ulysses, who enters with Telemachus, Laertes, Eumaeus, and his followers)

At last I'm pressing you in my arms!

ULYSSES:

(to Penelope)

Your wrongs are avenged, your tyrants are punished. (to Laertes)

Nothing will further afflict your august old age,

Father, and beautiful days will still be the reward

Of virtues whose example instructed my youth.

Let's render thanks to the gods who have reunited us.

PENELOPE:

Ah, what a moment for my tenderness!

ULYSSES, PENELOPE, TELEMACHUS, LAERTES:

(together)

Immortal gods! And you, Minerva, and you,

My tutelary Divinity

His tutelary divinity!

How many prayers! How many altars! How much incense I owe you!

ULYSSES:

Penelope!

LAERTES:

(to Ulysses) Ulysses!

ULYSSES:

(to Telemachus) My son!

PENELOPE:

Dear Ulysses!

TELEMACHUS:

(to Ulysses) My father!

THE FOUR:

I'm finally seeing you again!

Ah! How many charms for me

This day, this fine day which shines on me!

PENELOPE:

Ah! what wife! Ah! What mother

Will be happier than I am!

ULYSSES:

What son, what husband, and what father

Was ever as happy as I!

TELEMACHUS:

What son, in the arms of his father,

Was ever as happy as I!

PENELOPE AND LAERTES:

(to Ulysses)

What son, what husband, and what father

Was ever as beloved as you!

GENERAL CHORUS:

Immortal gods! And you, Minerva, and you,

His tutelary divinity!

Protect, defend, preserve, this good king.

A general ballet ends the Opera.

CURTAIN

SAPPHO
BY ÉMILE AUGIER,
Music by Charles Gounod

CAST OF CHARACTERS:

SAPPHO

GLYCERA

OENONE

PHAON

PYTHIAS

ALCAEUS

PITTACUS

CYNEGIRUS

CRATES

AGATHON

A SHEPHERD

ACT I
SCENE 1

At Olympia. A square before the temple of Jupiter. At the back, on one side of the stage, the temple whose façade and steps face the audience.

AT RISE, the crowd is proceeding in procession toward the temple.

PROCESSIONAL CHORUS:

O Jupiter, if you are pleased by games,

By sacred games that celebrate Olympia,

Don't permit the triumph of impiety;

Don't allow the courageous to be shamed!

(Enter the procession of an Athletic Victor.)

VICTOR'S CHORUS:

Mix the honey with barley!

Glory to the winner of three matches!

His rivals, shaken by the throat

Almost to death, won't forget

That the rough hammer of the forge

Is less terrible than his arm.

Mix the honey with barley!

Glory to the winner of three matches.

(The Victor's procession goes into the temple.)

PROCESSIONAL CHORUS:

Happy the one the crowd contemplates

And whose name is born up to the heavens.

Nothing is finer than a victor in a temple

Bending his glory at the feet of gods.

(The Processional Chorus enters the temple.)

PYTHIAS:

You are not following the multitude, Phaon.

PHAON:

I am better here.

PYTHIAS:

You are going to seem a fainthearted lover.

PHAON:

Lover, and why's that?

PYTHIAS:

Because, usually

Hearts gripped with solitude

Are not hearts without care.

PHAON:

Surely, I have some; but I imagine,

Good Pythias, that you are not lacking them

From the tyrant conspiring to ruin us.

PYTHIAS:

Pittacus and Lesbos are far away!

Let's forget for a minute

Lesbos, Pittacus, and his fall!

From Glycera you feel you've detached your heart,

And for Sappho—but what, already blushing?

So I guessed it?

PHAON:

I admit it!—

My heart is floating between two loves

And Venus maliciously delights

In seeing it distracted with its own twistings.

Can I forget, o my Glycera,

Our happy days,

So much grace and light

From your beautiful eyes,

Your beautiful dazzling shoulder

Under the necklace,

O Glycera, and your languishing voice—

Can I forget?

PYTHIAS:

If your memory is unfaithful,

A thousand nearby,

A thousand other lovers of the beauty

Will remember.

And Sappho?

PHAON:

Sappho!

Terrestrial body, divine soul,

Look conqueror!

Clay lamp that illuminates

The heart's fire!

Sappho, I am unaware by what charms

You retain me;

But I've seen your eyes full of tears

And recall them.

Yes, you remain in memory

For her love,

Glycera, your name was glorious

For a day!

VOICES OF MEN OF THE PEOPLE:

(at the back)

There's Sappho! Sappho! Sappho's coming!

Look!

PYTHIAS:

(to Phaon) When Glycera passes by

No one says anything at all.

PHAON:

Her naked feet are so beautiful on rugs from Sardis!

PYTHIAS:

And her cheek is so red when she paints it!

PEOPLE:

She's coming in, friends, stand up! Stand up!

(Sappho enters, followed by young girls.)

CHORUS:

Greetings, o rival of Alcaon!

Greetings, o muse of Lesbos!

As you were born you were caressed

By the God they adore at Delos!

SAPPHO:

Phaon! This meeting is a lucky omen.

PHAON:

All are moved by your passage. (aside)

At her glance I feel all my senses troubled. (aloud to Sappho)

Can my voice mix with so many voices?

SAPPHO:

With lyre and poetry I dispute the prize,

Not without fear, not without terror,

But I will enter the field more calmly

If I know your prayers are with me.

PHAON:

Ah! Sappho, my prayers and my soul!

GLYCERA:

(entering)

What sweet conversation keeps your soul so occupied,

Phaon, to forget yourself so far from me?

PHAON:

What do you want?

GLYCERA:

I see they didn't deceive me

And my place in your heart is near to being usurped.

PYTHIAS:

(aside) Good! The business is starting!

Let's listen, let's remain still!

SAPPHO:

(to Phaon) Who is that bold woman?

GLYCERA:

That woman! She's only a nameless woman

That the Greeks have not applauded,

That one takes and dismisses

Without even telling her the reason;

But however small she may be, she is proud, Phaon!

And she won't endure her lover giving her a rival

Were she Aphrodite in person.

PHAON:

(to Glycera)

You are listening to much pride from your attractions.

GLYCERA:

(to Phaon) Yes, I am listening to it and why not?

Do you think I will be confounded

By struggling with a muse?

If it's a question of love, I think that

The beauty of Asian girls

Is the first poetry,

And that was your opinion one day.

TOGETHER

PHAON:

When she urges me to choose,

It's necessary that by a mocking game,

Fate, weighing my tenderness,

Makes my heart hesitate!

PYTHIAS:

They fight over his tenderness,

Is he lucky, this conqueror!

And as for me, I shiver through the night

Without being able to dispose of my heart.

SAPPHO:

So he had a mistress

And I must fight for his heart!

Who cares? I will have his tenderness

With the victor's palm.

GLYCERA:

He dares to name his mistress;

But with the victorious memory

Of his passions and our intoxication

I will retain his heart!

(Chorus of priests enter, while people exit the temple, and take places at various points around the stage.)

CHORUS OF PRIESTS:

The entrails of sacrifices

Assure us that the gods

Are delighted.

Poets, be sublime!

Because your harmonious hymns

Are heard in the heavens.

O powerful Jupiter, O sovereign of gods,

Moderator of the world, assembler of clouds,

Drive away their dark troupe from the plain of the skies,

And exile storms to other climes.

THE PEOPLE:

Grant our prayers, O Jupiter,

Master of earth and air.

PRIESTS:

These divine poets are going to bring their honey to you;

If you are pleased by the games of these noble bees,

Command, king of the air, the four winds of heaven

To allow their songs to reach your ears!

THE PEOPLE:

Grant our prayers, O Jupiter!

Master of earth and air.

THE HIGH PRIEST:

The gods have seen our sacrifices with a clement eye.

TWO HERALDS:

O poets, sing, for the gods are propitious!

THE HERALD:

(on one of the steps of the temple)

Alcaeus! Alcaeus! Alcaeus!

ALCAEUS:

(coming forward to center stage, singing)

O Liberty, austere goddess,

They broke your proud altar;

But of your steps, old earth

Keeps an immortal memory.

There comes an hour when each fiber

Revolts in generous hearts

And shouts to man that he is free

And his only master is the gods.

Let the arm rise

For ills suffered;

In default of a sword

Let's brandish our chains.

Humanity that degenerates,

Isn't it still the child of gods?

Its eye lowered towards the dust,

Doesn't it dare look at the heavens?

So regrasp your heritage,

Noble race, with your pride.

If you were born into slavery

Bequeath liberty to your sons.

Let the arm rise

For wrongs endured;

In default of a sword

Let's brandish our chains.

THE PEOPLE:

Death to tyranny!

Misfortune to whoever dozes

In this shame!

Rather die!

ALCAEUS:

Do you hear them, Phaon, these shouts of happy omen?

PHAON:

Greece has understood you! It encourages us.

HERALD:

(on the steps of the altar) Sappho! Sappho! Sappho!

THE PEOPLE (distracted)

Silence! Listen!

SAPPHO:

(coming forward, and singing)

Hero, in her solitary tower,

Breathing freshness from the seas,

Awaits the nocturnal swimmer

That guides love toward land.

Trembling by the vault of the heavens

Phoebe spreads over the marine plain

A silvery caress

Of silent rays.

All sleep on the perfumed earth,

But in the heart of the beloved,

The night of love

Is broad daylight.

The sea that separates them is so vast and deep.

Time passes—he doesn't come.

But suddenly on the waves, his blond head shines

Yet quite distant—quite distant, alas!

But love sustains his courage

He advances, he's coming closer, he's reached the beach

And towards the tower his feet hurry.

Hero, pale and joyous, is finally in his arms!

Come in the arms of your lover

Audacious, conquering waves,

Come share the ardent passion

That lifts us to the rank of gods.

One day this beautiful flame,

Piercing the darkness of time,

Will give to our tender and faithful love

Immortality.

THE PEOPLE:

Evoë! Glory!

Evoë! Glory!

ALCAEUS:

I intend to proclaim your victory!

THE PEOPLE:

Evoë!

PYTHIAS:

O Glycera! O supreme beauty

I will have you!

THE PEOPLE:

Evoë!

PHAON:

(to Sappho) Every one admires you, and as for me, I love you.

SAPPHO:

Thanks, Venus, o protectrice!

You take pity on my torture

You inspire me with the conquering tone!

It's you who are smiling on my troubles!

And your power brings me

All my joy with his heart.

PHAON:

Joy, intoxicating and supreme,

Yes, it's you, you alone that I love

It's you, daughter of heavens,

Whose victorious name

The wild crowd

Carries up to heaven.

SAPPHO:

In this nation that greets me

It's you alone that I see;

In the shouts of the agitated crowd

I hear only your voice, Phaon.

THE PEOPLE:

Let a whole nation salute you.

And that, by us, your conquering name

Be lifted and praised to high heaven.

Honor! Honor! Honor!

                CURTAIN

ACT II
SCENE 2

Phaon's home at Lesbos. A large room closed at the back by curtains. To the left, placed obliquely, a long table covered with amphora, and cups of fruit. To the right, a round table with three legs beside an armchair. Chairs on both sides of the table at the left.

ALCAEUS:

Let's deliberate; the place and the time are propitious

For the party that Phaon is giving here to Sappho

Dissipates suspicions under these joyous auspices

And leaves tyranny's prudence in default.

Tomorrow, at dawn, he leaves with very few of his followers

For the hunt; it's we that he must find in ambush.

PYTHIAS:

(very moved) What! Tomorrow?

PHAON:

Yes! He's going to offer himself to our blows himself.

ALCAEUS:

Each of us has his assigned task

For the great day.

Before leaving, let's swear to accomplish it.

ALL:

We swear to accomplish everything,

Shame on him whose hand trembles!

Liberty, to conquer you

We shall conquer or die together!

PHAON:

Come see the queen of the fest.

Let's forget everything, friends, until tomorrow.

PYTHIAS:

(on the forestage as Phaon and the others are going to meet Sappho)

Before the peril that's being prepared,

Where to find forgetfulness? In wine!

(He sits at the table to the left and pours himself a drink.)

(Sappho enters with her women.)

PHAON:

Greetings, beautiful victor!

Your presence here

Fills me with joy and pride.

I will mark this happy day in red.

CHORUS:

We'll mark this happy day in red.

SAPPHO:

It's me, Lord, that your greeting

Fills with joy and pride.

CHORUS:

Greetings, beautiful victor!

(Pittacus enters with a servant who brings an ivory box.)

ALL:

Pittacus!

PHAON:

He!

PITTACUS:

(to Phaon) Does that surprise you?

I know that you are celebrating Sappho's victory,

And like a good tyrant, I rush

To offer my tribute to her glory. (to Sappho)

Muse, open this ivory box.

CHORUS:

A gold crown!

SAPPHO:

It's too much, Lord, you make me confused.

PITTACUS:

Say that it's too little! By Castor and Pollux

You deserve much more!

What wouldn't I have to offer you, O Muse,

A diadem instead of a simple laurel of gold!

SAPPHO:

O chaste sisters, wise troupe,

Worthy of being commended to the gods,

He who respects the pious

Honors you in your servant.

PITTACUS:

The gods are listening to you—if they listen to anyone. (to Phaon)

In favor of its purpose, excuse my visit,

Lord, now I am leaving you,

Not wishing to be importunate.

ALCAEUS:

(to Sappho) Suffer Phaon to invite him in your name.

SAPPHO:

Surely.

PITTACUS:

(to Phaon) You are quiet?

PHAON:

(bowing) She is queen here.

PITTACUS:

(offering his hand to Sappho) Well, let's crown her!

SAPPHO:

Noble Lords, thanks!

(Pittacus escorts her to the back of the stage surrounded by women; meanwhile, they place the crown on her head, and the conspirators reassemble to the left and sing on the sly.)

PYTHIAS:

Now he's putting his head

In the jaws of the wolf.

ALCAEUS:

Let's embloody the feast.

ANOTHER:

Let him fall under our blows!

PHAON:

So long as he's under my roof, he's sacred to us all!

(Pittacus escorts Sappho to the chair near the round table to the right and remains standing behind her.)

ALCAEUS:

(to Phaon) To spare him, what a sin!

PHAON:

(filling cups, sends one by a slave to Pittacus, and raises the other.)

I drink to you, my guest. (turning towards the conspirators)

I drink the wine of hospitality!

CHORUS:

To hospitality!

PITTACUS:

And as for me, Sappho, I drink to immortality.

CHORUS:

To immortality!

Glory to Bacchus, god of the winecup!

Glory to Bacchus, god of good wine!

For us, he stole the divine juice

From the celestial troupe!

(During this chorus Pittacus speaks in a low voice to Sappho; Phaon observes them suspiciously.)

ALCAEUS:

He wanted that when a man weeps,

Saddened by the burdens of life,

For each to procure

An hour of divinity!

CHORUS:

Glory to Bacchus, etc.

PHAON:

My eye is bothered, a sweet mystery

Transports me among the gods;

When what you see is no longer earthly,

Doubtless, what you see is heavenly!

CHORUS:

Glory to Bacchus, etc.

PITTACUS:

But, as for you, Pythias, with reddened face

You are drinking a lot and saying nothing!

PHAON:

Come on! To reawaken your slumbering frivolity,

The song to Bacchus!

PYTHIAS:

Indeed! I'd really like to.

(Pythias opens his lips with difficulty; Pittacus notices it by smiling to Sappho.)

PYTHIAS:

Let Mars renounce our homage!

We'll skip this god,

Bacchus is the god of courage,

For he alone gives it to cowards!

Friends, a drunk is worth four men

A soldier fasting is paralyzed.

Thanks, Bacchus,

No more worries!

Through you I've succeeded in emboldening myself!

Let's drink, friends, let's drink! If it's a question of fighting,

Seeing double is the best way of striking twice as hard.

Venus is no longer a goddess,

To Bacchus we are carrying her powers!

He's the true god of tenderness

For he alone gives it to the frigid!

Friends, a drunk is worth four men!

A lover fasting is paralyzed.

Thanks, Bacchus!

Through you I've succeeded in emboldening myself!

Let's drink, friends, let's drink! If it's a question of fighting,

Seeing double is the best way of striking twice as hard.

(He sits back down near the table in the midst of the laughter and applause of those present.)

PHAON:

And now, Lords, let's go into the gardens

Where chatting about all things

Under flowering myrtles and oleanders

We will gaily await the hour of buffoons.

Sappho! Lords! Deign to follow me!

PITTACUS:

Save Pythias! For he is drunk!

(All leave)

PYTHIAS:

Yes, tyrant, I am drunk, but not sufficiently yet

To tell you the degree to which your life is threatened.

GLYCERA:

(entering enveloped in a thick veil, without seeing Pythias)

Cymbals and cithers

Make my shame ring in the air,

In delightful fanfares

From my eyes I bring lightning to Phaon!

—Pythias?

PYTHIAS:

You, Glycera?

GLYCERA:

And why not? Where are they?

PYTHIAS:

By Bacchus,

You have the air of a panther!

GLYCERA:

Where are they?

PYTHIAS:

(pointing to the gardens) With Pittacus.

GLYCERA:

Pittacus here?

PYTHIAS:

Without an escort.

Reckless!

GLYCERA:

(astonished) Reckless?

PYTHIAS:

No question. Unfortunately,

Hospitality protects him.

GLYCERA:

Against what?

PYTHIAS:

(trying to get out of it) Against—the heat!

GLYCERA:

Who invited him?

PYTHIAS:

Nobody—

He brought a crown.

GLYCERA:

(bitterly) For the muse?

PYTHIAS:

Yes, in that box.

(Pointing to it on the round table where the slave of Pittacus has placed it.)

GLYCERA:

Thus her triumph is complete!

Oh! I hate her! Who will avenge me on her?

Who will avenge me on Phaon?

PYTHIAS:

Forget your faithless lover

And avenge yourself in a fine way

By letting me gather from your—cheek—

GLYCERA:

(pushing him away) You are drunk.

PYTHIAS:

I admit it.

A little, but not yet sufficiently

To tell him to what degree his life is threatened.

GLYCERA:

Assuredly, something is being plotted.

(She heads toward the table.)

PYTHIAS:

(following her)

Oh! How beautiful she is, this woman!

GLYCERA:

(taking a cup and pouring a drink for Pythias from an amphora)

Let's drink to the success of the conspiracy!

PYTHIAS:

(speechless) Of what conspiracy?

GLYCERA:

The one Pythias is the ringleader of.

PYTHIAS:

(falling into a seat near the table)

Me? To conspire is not my lot.

GLYCERA:

So much the worse!

Such audacity in you would have pleased me!

PYTHIAS:

I would please her with such audacity.

(Pythias drinks, Glycera fills the cup.)

GLYCERA:

And you would have made yourself handsome on the spot!

PYTHIAS:

I would seem handsome on the spot!

(Pythias drinks, Glycera pours again.)

GLYCERA:

For valor is men is elegant!

PYTHIAS:

Yes, valor is our elegance.

(Pythias drinks, Glycera pours again.)

GLYCERA:

And I don't know all that I would have done!

PYTHIAS:

(rising) I understand all that she would have done!

TOGETHER:

GLYCERA (aside) Soon, a bit of hope,

I think, is going to

Make him indiscreet.

I've got my vengeance

If I have their secret!

PYTHIAS (aside) O sweet hope,

For my imprudence!

What! I will please her

By confiding

All our secrets!

PYTHIAS:

(mysteriously) Well, it's necessary to tell you

Since you are provoking me

Tomorrow, Pittacus will expire!

GLYCERA:

(sitting by the table where the ivory box is)

You are having fun?

PYTHIAS:

(on the other side of the table) No—on the way to the hunt

We will all be in ambush

And bad luck to him if he comes by!

GLYCERA:

You are having fun!

PYTHIAS:

By the Styx! Must you be told

All the names of the conspirators?

Phaon, Crates, Cynegirus—

GLYCERA:

You are having fun.

PYTHIAS:

Alcaeus, Alcidamas, Aegisthus!

GLYCERA:

I don't believe a thing!

PYTHIAS:

(pulling a notebook from his breast) Here's the list

From the very hand of Phaon

And you can see my name there. (gives her the notebooks and stretches his hand to take it back)

Do you still doubt?

GLYCERA:

No!

(Placing her right hand in Pythias' extended hand, and keeping the notebook in her left.)

GLYCERA:

Go, wait for me, my master!

Go, shut the window

Light your tripod

I will go, dressed in rose

To join you at night's end

On tiptoe!

PYTHIAS:

(kissing the hand she holds) Yes, I love your caprice

With candor!

The mystery is abetted

With joy!

GLYCERA:

Go, wait for me, my master, etc.

TOGETHER:

Goodbye! Something mysterious!

Wait until night

I'll wait until night

Has extinguished on earth

Daylight and noise.

(Pythias leaves staggering.)

GLYCERA:

(alone) I prefer to see him dead than happy with my rival!

Ah! Those who are suffering are evil! (her eyes rest on the small table)

That box suggests an infernal idea to me

A double-edged vengeance (writing on Pythias' tablets)

"Guard yourself, Lord, they're plotting.

Here's the names of the conspirators.

Their plans are already prepared

In the regions where the hunt must lead you tomorrow.

Screen yourself from their fury

And guess your savior."

(She places the notebooks in the box.)

GLYCERA:

O the sensual delight of satisfied hate!

Subtleties of vengeance in return

You bring to my ravished heart

More intoxication than love!

I savor you, bitter delight

With a rapidly beating heart!

I am going to inflict on my rival a torture

That will surpass her happiness!

Go, accursed, strut,

Crowned and serene.

You think this triumph of one day is eternal?

A sudden bolt of lightning

Will soon burst in the blue azure of your heaven!

(She leaves by the right taking the box under her arm.)

CURTAIN

ACT II
SCENE 3

The stage represents the gardens of Phaon.

SAPPHO:

(descending at the rear with her cortege)

In this abode, my life is a limpid stream.

Which spreads on the moss and reflects light.

Let's love, my sisters, let's love, for life is rapid

And time is wasted that passes without love.

PITTACUS:

Friend, Phaon, this feast is magnificent!

I love to see you seized by dance and music.

PHAON:

It's better than troubling ourselves

With public policies?

You are here to think of it?

PITTACUS:

You speak goldenly!

PHAON:

Pooh on politics!

Let's sit down: the choruses are going to begin.

(All are seated. The ballet enters.)

CURTAIN

ACT III
SCENE 4

Sappho's home. A locked room. A statue of Apollo towards the left.

One of the women hangs the crown of the second act at the feet of Apollo.

SAPPHO:

What are you doing?

WOMAN:

I'm hanging this crown here

While waiting for the slave Agathon

To bring back the ivory box forgotten at Phaon's.

SAPPHO:

He's really slow, my dear Oenone.

WOMAN:

Here he is.

(Enter Agathon.)

SAPPHO:

What a distracted air!

AGATHON:

Ah! Madame! What an adventure!

Phaon's palace is surrounded by soldiers,

Himself, in flight, they assure us

A conspiracy discovered and all the conspirators

Captured, except Phaon!

THE WOMEN:

Great Gods! What an adventure!

SAPPHO:

(kneeling before the statue)

Immortal gods in whom I have faith,

Let my prayer reach you.

If his love was too much a blessing for me

Take his love away from me, but let him live!

THE WOMEN:

Save Phaon, immortal gods,

And we will flower your altars!

(Phaon enters.)

SAPPHO:

Phaon! (to her women) Leave us alone. And you at the gate, Agathon;

Let no one enter or leave.

(They all leave.)

PHAON:

Learn that—

SAPPHO:

I know everything.

PHAON:

(astonished) Everything? And from whom?

SAPPHO:

Never mind!

What are you doing here? You will ruin yourself!

Leave, wretch, leave quickly!

They told me you were in flight.

PHAON:

All the passages are guarded,

You cannot leave the city.

SAPPHO:

Then stay hidden in my house.

PHAON:

I am not coming to ask you asylum.

Surrounded by treason,

Resistance is useless.

I came to say my goodbyes to you

Before giving myself up.

Keep a pious memory

Of this wretch who loves you!

SAPPHO:

If you love me, save yourself

For me, cruel one, for me!

PHAON:

I am lost: what remains to me

To save on this funereal day

Is the dignity of defeat.

In an hour I will have died,

But let me fall under the ax

Intrepidly, and not as a coward!

SAPPHO:

Ingrate, have you no pride?

Mine is humiliating itself before you;

I am kneeling and I supplicate you,

Don't put my love in mourning!

Resist the pride that urges you

To rush to your fate,

And don't prevent my tenderness

From battling death over you!

PHAON:

Gods sustain me in this test,

My virtue is ready to collapse!

SAPPHO:

I insist on this proof of your love!

If, despite all, I cannot save you

At least allow me, allow me as your widow,

To preserve this memory.

PHAON:

My widow! You?

SAPPHO:

(her eyes lowered)

I was destined for you.

Remain hidden—let a secret marriage—

PHAON:

O heaven! (throwing himself at her knees and holding her in his arms)

Let's intoxicate ourselves with our love!

In one kiss, let's swallow life

And let death, in its turn find

The cup drained

By our thirst on a sole and last day.

SAPPHO:

Remain hidden—

Our marriage

Will deflect destiny

And to strike you in my arms

No! Death won't dare.

TOGETHER

SAPPHO, PHAON:

Let's intoxicate ourselves with our love!

In one kiss let's swallow life!

And let death, in its turn find

The cup drained

By our thirst on a sole and last day!

AGATHON:

(entering) The street is full of soldiers

And Pittacus is on my heels.

PHAON:

Already! You see, he's come to get me.

SAPPHO:

Ah! Let me protect you to the end.

(She pushes him toward the curtain; he takes her in his arms and kisses her face and vanishes behind the curtain. Sappho turns smiling towards Pittacus, who enters, in armor, helmet in hand, followed by several soldiers who remain at the door outside.)

SAPPHO:

What! Lord, you at my place? What a favor!

PITTACUS:

Did I guess my savior?

SAPPHO:

Your savior?

(Enter Glycera. She hides behind the statue.)

PITTACUS:

O ingenuous surprise—

But it's necessary to remain unknown

To find a more discreet messenger,

Madame, than this particular box.

GLYCERA:

(aside) My ruse succeeded!

SAPPHO:

(to Pittacus) Doubtless, you are jesting

Because I don't understand.

PITTACUS:

Is someone listening to us?

SAPPHO:

(excitedly) No one!

PITTACUS:

Why pretend then? What is this game?

SAPPHO:

(turning her eyes towards Phaon's hiding place.) Nobody!

GLYCERA:

(aside) Fine! Phaon is there.

PITTACUS:

Let's break the mirror.

To whoever denounced the conspiracy, I made a vow

To grant a grace.

GLYCERA:

(aside) I've got her! Nemesis is leading her under my blows.

SAPPHO:

Well, Lord?

PITTACUS:

Well, what do you request of me?

SAPPHO:

Me! It's me they accuse—

Oh, what infamy!

PITTACUS:

Simply of being my friend.

I am coming to repay your kindness. (Glycera appears on stage)

You see plainly someone was listening. (Glycera falls at his feet)

Who is this?

SAPPHO:

(aside) What audacity!

GLYCERA:

(to Pittacus) It's the mistress of Phaon,

Coming to ask mercy for him!

PITTACUS:

What service have you done me, what is your name,

For daring to ask of me impunity for crime?

GLYCERA:

Noble Lord, be magnanimous!

PITTACUS:

(raising her up) Mercy for Phaon? Never!

SAPPHO:

And if I asked it of you?

PITTACUS:

That's different: as for you, I owe you my life

And I took a vow which binds me.

GLYCERA:

(aside, turning toward the curtain that hides Phaon)

And what's more, Phaon, who you are not expecting!

PITTACUS:

Let your will be done.

Is this enough to pay my debt to you?

SAPPHO:

Yes, Lord, my prayer has penetrated the heavens.

GLYCERA:

Mine, too. Let's render thanks to the gods.

TOGETHER

GLYCERA:

To your confessions I have bound you.

It's Phaon who received them,

You can't be exalted by 'em

I ask nothing more.

SAPPHO:

To my confessions I am bound.

It's Phaon who received them,

You can be exalted by 'em

I ask nothing more.

PITTACUS:

Her conduct is badly motivated

From the admissions I've received

But still my life is saved.

I ask nothing more.

PITTACUS:

(to Sappho) Then let him live! But his presence

On Lesbos creates a peril for me

That exceeds my gratitude.

Do you accept exile for him?

PHAON:

(rushing on stage) Take my head!

(Pittacus places his hand on his sword.)

PHAON:

Leave your hasty sword in its furrow.

I am without arms before you

As you were yesterday in my home.

I've lost, take the wager!

Let the executioner get ready!

PITTACUS:

(to Sappho)

You were hiding the author of the denounced conspiracy?

SAPPHO:

Lord, I wanted to save the one and the other—

GLYCERA:

(to Pittacus, who turns towards her undecided)

So as to have a clean conscience?

PITTACUS:

(making a gesture of assent and turning towards Phaon)

As you were listening, you heard—

PHAON:

Yes, that the lady betrayed me.

PITTACUS:

But she also bought you back.

PHAON:

(to Sappho) And by what right? Do you think that after betrayal

I still have a desire to live?

Death, exile or prison.

I chose death which frees.

PITTACUS:

Phaon, you don't have a choice.

PHAON:

(to Sappho) Wretch! What thought

Pushed you into such a crime?

Were you hoping to

Change this crown into a diadem?

(Phaon tears the crown suspended from the pedestal and it rolls at her feet.)

SAPPHO:

(aside) He thinks!

GLYCERA:

(aside) Fine! Everything suits blaming her.

PITTACUS:

(aside) Indeed, who knows? Woman, what a puzzle!

SAPPHO:

(aside)

Great gods, at what a price you are selling me my salvation!

PHAON:

(striding back) Well, no! It's not possible

No! You didn't betray us!

Wake me from a horrible dream!

Swear to me it wasn't you!

SAPPHO:

(with spirit) Ah, I swear—

(Glycera stops her by touching her shoulder; she turns and finds herself face to face with Pittacus.)

PITTACUS:

Go on, finish.

SAPPHO:

I swear it was me.

TOGETHER:

SAPPHO:

O cruel sacrifice!

Must I submit

To pay his ransom

With this horrible torture!

This horrible suspicion!

PITTACUS:

From interest or caprice

You rendered me a service

But treachery

My beautiful protectress

Doesn't open my home.

GLYCERA:

O blessing! O delight!

Thanks to my artifice

To pay his ransom

She has to submit

To this horrible suspicion!

PHAON:

O you, gods of justice!

Ought I to see

The like treachery!

Such a cruel torture

Distracts my reason.

PITTACUS:

You will leave tomorrow for the Bosporus.

PHAON:

Your clemency dishonors me.

I want to share the misfortune of my friends.

PITTACUS:

But your reprieve entails theirs.

I'm embarking you all on the same ship

Saving them with you, you have nothing to say.

(Phaon lowers his head.)

GLYCERA:

As for me, I have something to say!

PITTACUS:

(smiling) Really?

GLYCERA:

I was part of the conspiracy: I surrender.

PHAON:

(low to Glycera) That's not true!

GLYCERA:

(low) I want to follow you!

SAPPHO:

Ah! This is too much.

PITTACUS:

(to Glycera) Yes, too much devotion.

GLYCERA:

(pointing to Sappho) The lady has less, I confess

For this exile to which I am devoting myself. (to Phaon)

It's to her that you owe it.

PHAON:

Alas!

SAPPHO:

(aside) When all my heart is rushing towards my lips,

I must condemn myself by my silence!

GLYCERA:

(to Phaon) I want to attach myself to your heels,

Accept me as your servant. (to Pittacus)

I was in the plot, and I am proud of it.

Lord, don't separate us!

PHAON:

(to Sappho) You hear her, Lady? (to Glycera) Come with me, come noble lady!

TOGETHER

PITTACUS:

The girl with blue eyes

Truly interests me.

If she's his mistress

The monster is lucky!

PHAON:

(to Glycera) We are leaving these parts!

In parting I am leaving

To this traitress

Forgetfulness for goodbyes!

GLYCERA:

(to Phaon) Come, let's leave these parts.

Let your pride leave

To this traitress

Oblivion for goodbyes!

SAPPHO:

Is it enough, great gods!

I am losing his tenderness,

Another mistress

Is leading him away before my eyes!

PITTACUS:

(to his soldiers who remain at the back)

Soldiers, take the two of them away.

(Phaon and Glycera leave between four soldiers. Pittacus follows them. Sappho falls crushed at the foot of the statue.)

CURTAIN

ACT IV
SCENE 5

Rocks on the seashore. The sun is going down.

SAPPHO:

(alone) This is the funereal vessel awaiting its prey.

I must see you one last time. (the orchestra recall the Romance of Phaon at the beginning of the first act)

Why these memories of my lost happiness

When my soul is in mourning and weeping?

What do you expect of me at this time,

Echoes of a song heard so many times? (she takes the lyre and accompanies herself)

Terrestrial body, divine soul,

Conquering look,

The silver lamp that ignites

The heart's fire.

Sappho, I am unaware through what charms

You keep me

But I've seen your eyes filled with tears

And I remember!

(Glycera enters from the right followed by slaves bearing boxes.)

SAPPHO:

Her again!

GLYCERA:

Is this your place or mine?

Is it you who is leading Phaon away?

They allowed me to take a head start

With some of my men

To embark this world of finery

Without which our allures are so uncertain!

The tyrant understood that I still intend

Even in exile to do my lord and master proud.

(Sappho moves away disdainfully without answering. Glycera throws herself in front of her, barring her way.)

GLYCERA:

Ah! This is too much insolence!

I understand your silence,

Your scorn is inward.

But I have the right to your hate

And with a word, noble queen,

I will make you gnash your teeth!

(Sappho shrugs her shoulders and takes some steps, but Glycera follows her.)

GLYCERA:

It's I who, from the need of a gnawing vengeance,

Betrayed the conspiracy and managed

To have you accused of this treachery.

SAPPHO:

Wretch!

GLYCERA:

Do you think that I am well avenged?

In your turn do you feel the shiver of hate?

SAPPHO:

But you are very imprudent

To take me for your confidant!

GLYCERA:

You'll repeat my confession

To Phaon? I consent to it; try!

I will deny everything; he won't believe you!

Truth without witnesses isn't true.

Anyway, you convinced him too well with your oath.

Am I an enemy to be despised,

What do you say to that, tenth muse?

SAPPHO:

O twice and thrice be wretched!

GLYCERA:

Insult is allowed to the vanquished.

SAPPHO:

You've defeated me, yes, glory in it!

But know, after such battles

That Sappho wouldn't exchange

Her defeat for your victory!

GLYCERA:

Hey! Who cares by what means

Your rival tears your soul out.

To your eyes I am less infamous

Than you are execrable to mine.

TOGETHER

SAPPHO:

Never, at the price of the greatest treasures

Would I want it, no! On my soul

To be as cowardly infamous

To your eyes as you are to mine.

GLYCERA:

Who cares by what means, etc.

(After the ensemble, Phaon enters with the conspirators escorted by the soldiers of Pittacus. Glycera and Sappho remain on the other side of the stage hidden behind some rocks.)

CHORUS OF CONSPIRATORS:

Goodbye, fatherland,

Cherished land,

You that your sons were unable to save.

Far from the shore so dear to their infancy.

Your avengers are going to preserve themselves

For the day of your deliverance. (turning towards the soldiers)

Mercenaries from Thrace,

Less soldiers than armed robbers,

Tremble! We will be back,

Driving out those who drive us out,

To the roar of our trumpets.

Mercenaries from Thrace,

We will meet you again

Goodbye, fatherland—etc.

(They head towards the rear between two files of soldiers and disappear amongst the rocks. Phaon marches behind them. Glycera retains him, pointing to Sappho.)

GLYCERA:

There's Sappho coming to say a last goodbye

To her victim.

PHAON:

Of Pittacus

Let her demand a diadem.

As for me, I no longer know her.

I detest her and scorn her,

With all the respect and love

With which my soul was seized

And that she betrayed on that day;

I have pity for what this false

And ambitious heart meditates.

Perfidious one, be thrice cursed

And I doom you to the gods of hell!

(He rejoins the other conspirators; some soldiers who were waiting for them bring up the procession.)

SAPPHO:

(alone) Be blessed by one dying!

If my prayer reaches the gods

Let their bounty watch over you from the height of the heavens

And protect your wandering life.

PHAON:

(and the conspirators in the distance) Goodbye, country,

Cherished land!

SAPPHO:

(screams and falls in a faint)

A HERDSMAN:

(descending the rocks at the back and crossing the stage singing)

Browse on thyme, browse, my goats,

Wild thyme, with thyme.

Blonde Aglaea with her lips

Touched mine this morning;

And I'm waiting for Venus to rise

To rejoin her on the shore.

Shine now, star of love,

And extinguish daylight in the heavens. (he disappears)

SAPPHO:

(alone, coming to) Where am I? Ah, yes, I remember.

Everything that tied me to life is shattered,

Nothing remains for me but eternal night

To rest my heart from consuming torture. (she takes her lyre)

O my immortal harp

That in these bad times

Amidst all my ills always

Faithfully consoled them!

Vainly your sweet murmurs

Want to help my suffering.

No, you cannot cure

My latest wound,

My wound is to the heart,

Death alone can end my sorrow!

Goodbye, torch of the world!

Descend to the breast of the waves!

As for me, I am descending beneath the ocean

Into eternal rest.

Day which must dawn

Will shine on you, Phaon,

But without thinking of me

You'll see the dawn again.

Open bitter gulf,

I am going to sleep forever in the sea. (she climbs the rock at the back; reaching the top, she repeats her last verse)

Open, bitter gulf,

I am going to sleep forever in the sea.

(She hurls herself off the rock.)

CURTAIN

ABOUT THE EDITOR

Frank J. Morlock has written and translated many plays since retiring from the legal profession in 1992. His translations have also appeared on Project Gutenberg, the Alexandre Dumas Père web page, Literature in the Age of Napoléon, Infinite Artistries.com, and Munsey's (formerly Blackmask). In 2006 he received an award from the North American Jules Verne Society for his translations of Verne's plays. He lives and works in México.

www.ingramcontent.com/pod-product-compliance
Lightning Source LLC
LaVergne TN
LVHW041618070426
835507LV00008B/318